INVASION!

The
Saxons

KAREN BRYANT-MOLE

Wayland

Invasion

The Saxons
The Vikings
The Normans
The Romans

Invasion! The Saxons is based on *Saxon Invaders and Settlers* by Tony D. Triggs, published by Wayland (Publishers) Ltd in 1992.

Picture acknowledgements
Ancient Art and Architecture Collection *Cover* (Left top and bottom), 22 (bottom left), 24 (bottom), 25 (bottom), 30; © Crown copyright 1995 MoD. Reproduced with the permisssion of the Controller of HMSO 27 (top); C M Dixon *Cover* (right top and bottom), Title page, Contents page (bottom and middle), 4 (top), 5, 17 (bottom), 18, 20 (bottom), 21 (bottom), 25, 31; E T Archives Limited 26; Michael Holford 15, 20 (top), 21 (top and middle), 22 (top), 28; St Paul's Jarrow Development Trust 23 (bottom right); West Stow Anglo-Saxon Village Trust *Contents page* (top), 7, 9, 11, 12, 13 (top and bottom), 16, 17 (top). The artwork on pages 4, 10-11, 14-15, 18, 24, 26, 27, 29 (right) is by Peter Bull, and pages 6, 8, 12, 19, 23 is by Peter Dennis, and page 29 (left) is by R. Mooney.

Cover design: Simon Balley
Book design: Malcolm Walker
Editor: Deb Elliott

First published in 1995 by
Wayland (Publishers) Limited,
61 Western Road, Hove, East Sussex, BN3 1JD

British Library Cataloguing in Publication Data
  Bryant-Mole, Karen
  Saxon Invaders. – (Invasion! Series)
  I. Title II. Series
  942.01

ISBN 0 7502 1468 6

Typeset by Kudos Editorial Services, England
Printed in Italy

Cover pictures
Top left: A gold clasp found at the Sutton Hoo ship burial in East Anglia.
Bottom left: A coin of King Alfred the Great (871–899).
Top right: A bird ornament on a shield, from the Sutton Hoo ship burial.
Bottom right: An Anglo-Saxon ivory showing a scribe writing a book.

Title page picture: A gold clasp from a burial mound in East Anglia.

Opposite page pictures
Top: Saxon coins found in East Anglia
Middle: A priory built on the site of a Saxon monastery.
Bottom: A reconstruction of King Redwald's helmet.

Contents

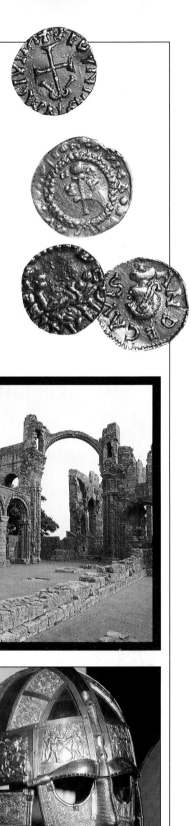

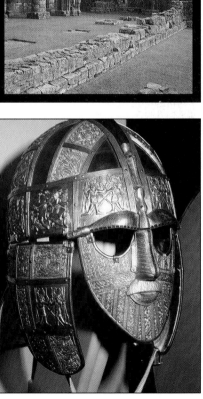

The Saxons

The Saxons began arriving in Britain from northern Europe from around the beginning of the fifth century.

Although they are known as the Saxons, they were actually a mixture of several different groups of people that included Jutes and Angles as well as Saxons.

▲ Before the Saxons settled in Britain, the country was run by the Romans. This picture shows part of Hadrian's Wall, which was built by the Romans.

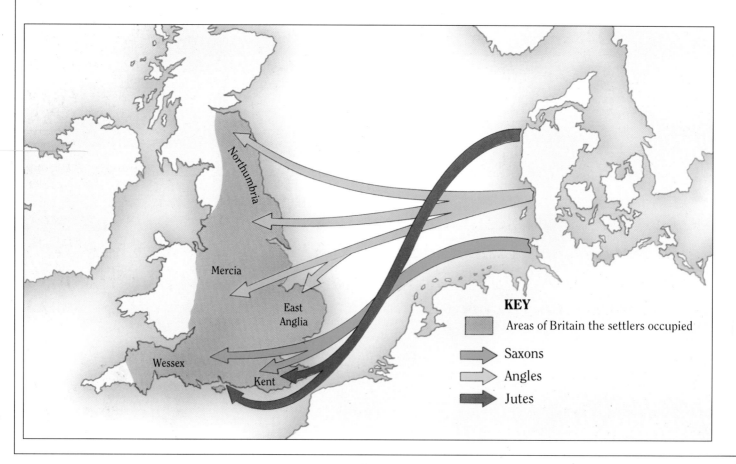

Northumbria

Mercia

East Anglia

Wessex

Kent

KEY

Areas of Britain the settlers occupied

→ Saxons

→ Angles

→ Jutes

When the Romans ruled Britain, they built forts, like this one, to defend the country against other invaders. In AD 383 the Roman army began to leave Britain. By AD 410 all the Roman armies had left and the Britons were left to defend themselves.

▲ A Saxon father gives his land to his eldest son. The younger son sets off to find his own land, perhaps in Britain.

Some people think that the Saxons may have come to Britain because Saxon fathers gave all their land to their eldest sons. Younger sons had to find new land for themselves by going to another country.

Other people think that the Saxons were raiders, who began by stealing gold and other treasure from Britain, but then decided to settle.

Village life

Saxon villages were usually surrounded by a strong, wooden fence to keep out raiders and wild animals. Inside the fence was a mixture of houses, huts, barns and workshops.

▼ This is where a large Saxon house once stood. The walls of the house were made from wood. The holes in the soil show where large wooden posts stood. Wood rots, so there are now no original Saxon houses left.

The huts in a village were often built in small groups. Each group probably belonged to one family. Saxon families often included lots of relatives.

▲ West Stow was a Saxon village. This house has been rebuilt to look like an original Saxon house.

Make a Saxon building

You will need an old shoe box and some long, thin pieces of wood.

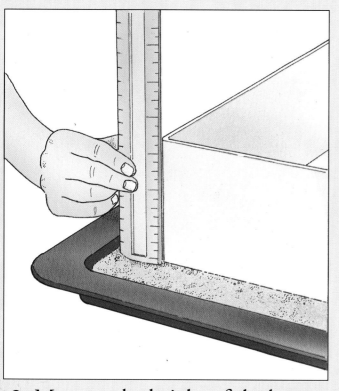

1 Cut a doorway in the box. Place the box on a tray filled with sand.

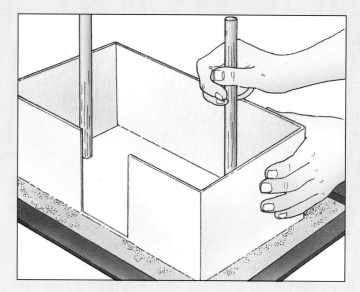

3 Cut two pieces of wood about two and a half times the height of the box. Push them through the box and into the sand.

2 Measure the height of the box.

4 Cut a third piece of wood so that it is the same length as the box. Glue it to the top of the other pieces.

▲ Rebuilding a Saxon house.

6 Use more card to fill in the space at each end. Paint the walls to look like wood and the roof to look like straw.

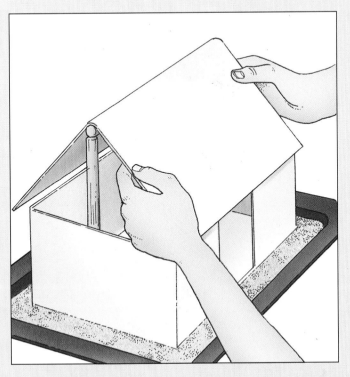

5 Make a sloping roof from card.

7 Use Plasticine to make a model family and fire.

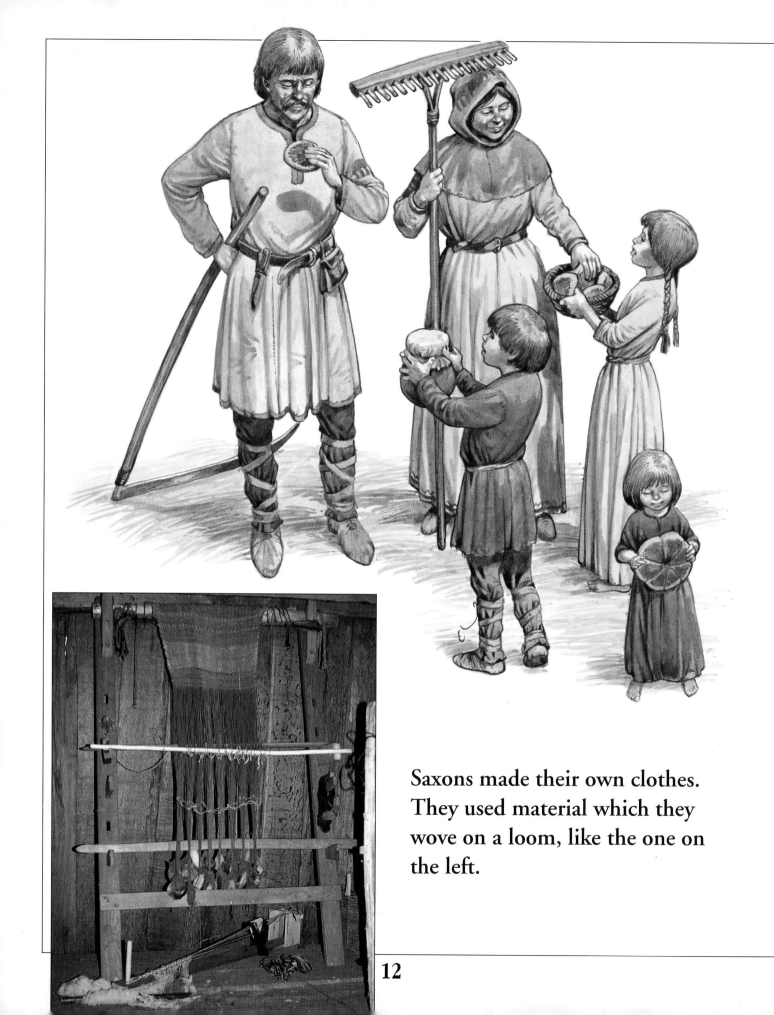

Saxons made their own clothes.
They used material which they
wove on a loom, like the one on
the left.

12

► These clay rings were used to weigh down threads on a loom. The needles were used to weave other threads in and out, from one side to the other.

The Saxons were very good at making clay pots. They used them for cooking and for storing and serving food and drink.

▼ Inside a Saxon hall. Saxon houses were smaller than the halls.

Make a Saxon pot

You will need some modelling clay or modelling dough.

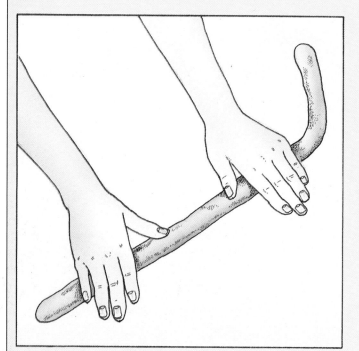

1 Roll the clay into a long 'snake'.

3 Roll out some more 'snakes'. Use them to make the sides of your pot.

2 Coil the 'snake' round. This will be the base of the pot.

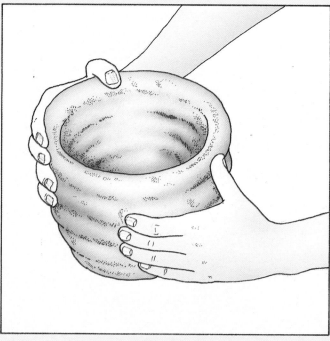

4 Smooth out the clay so that there are no cracks.

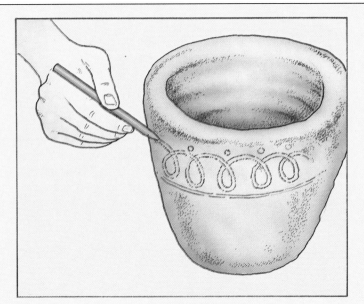

5 You could use a modelling tool to draw your own pattern.

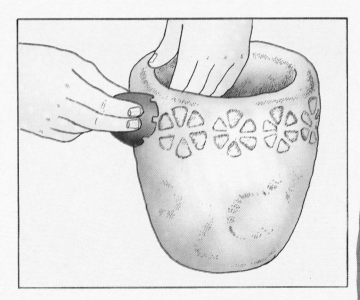

6 The Saxons sometimes decorated their pots by pressing an object with a raised design into the clay. You could try this, too.

▼ A Saxon clay pot.

Burials

When Saxons died, their bodies were either buried or burned to ashes.

People were usually buried with some of their belongings. This bronze brooch was found at West Stow. It may have been used to fasten a woman's dress.

Many bronze brooches have been found, so they were probably quite cheap. Rich Saxons had jewellery made from silver, gold and precious jewels.

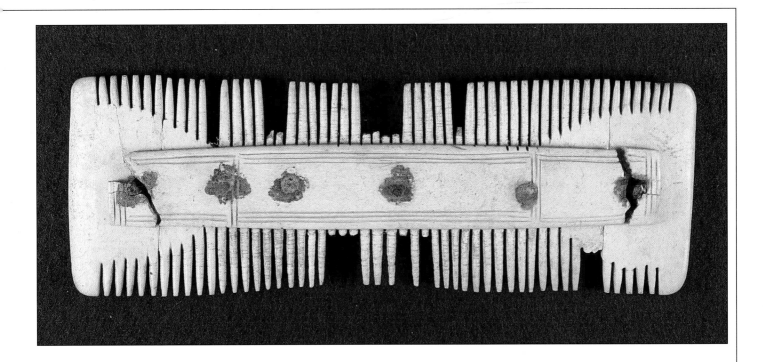

This pot was made for a dead person's ashes. The writing around the top is in a type of lettering called runes.

Small objects, like the comb above, would have been placed in the pot along with the ashes. Then the pot would have been buried.

A royal burial

The most important Saxon burial site ever found in Britain is in East Anglia, at a place called Sutton Hoo.

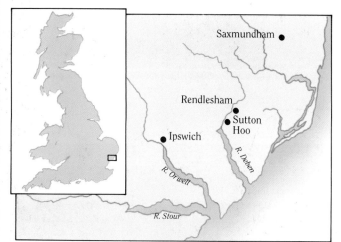

Grassy mounds show where the graves are. In 1939, the biggest mound was opened by archaeologists. Inside, they discovered that a Saxon ship had been buried there (see picture). Although the ship itself had rotted away, the archaeologists found a treasure trove of precious objects, like the gold clasp below.

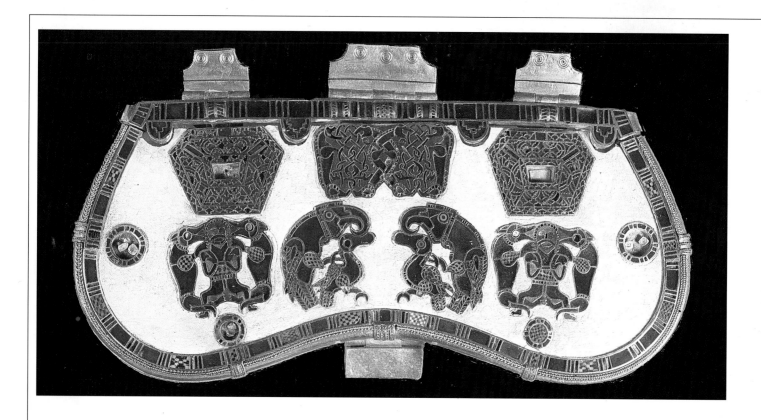

The picture above shows a purse lid. The coins at the bottom of the opposite page were found near the lid.

The picture on the left shows what the helmet of King Redwald might have been like. King Redwald was the King of East Anglia and the most important king in England at that time.

Pieces of a helmet were found in King Redwald's grave. The pieces were fitted together to make this helmet.

The beautiful dragon pictured below was part of a shield. Most of the shield was made from wood, which has rotted away.

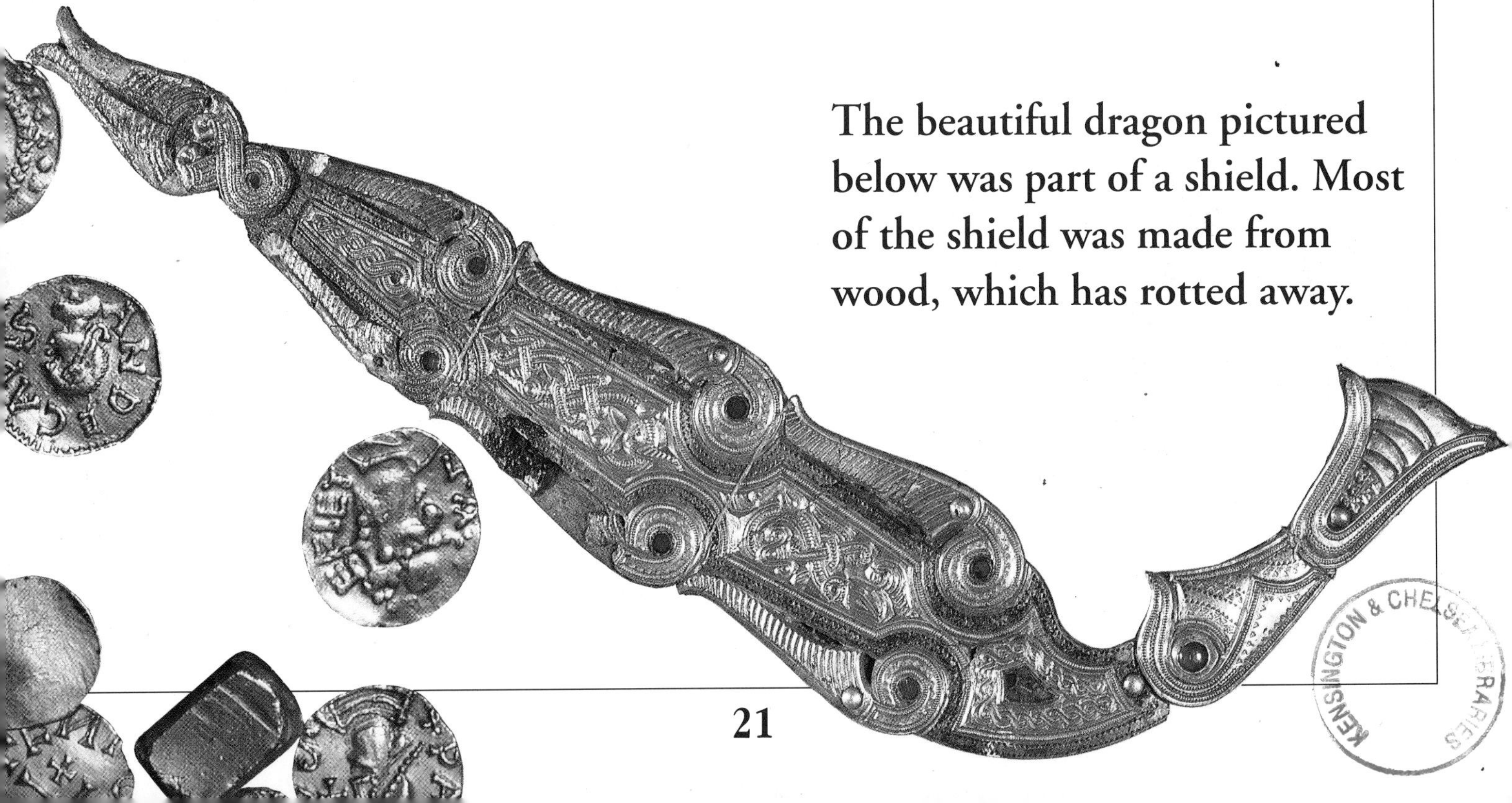

21

Christianity

▲ A church built in Saxon times.

The Saxon settlers did not believe in God. However, there were some groups of Christians living in Ireland and Wales. These Christians built monasteries in Scotland and the north of England and began telling people about Jesus.

Other Christians came to southern England from Europe. Gradually, most of the country became Christian.

At first, people gathered outside around crosses, like the one on the left, to pray. Later, people built churches.

► This is a model of a monastery in the north of England.

▲ These people are listening to a Christian preacher.

ᚠ = æ	= a	= b	ᚲ = c	= d	= e	= f	= g	= h	= i
ᛄ = j	ᚴ = k	= l	= m	= n	ᛝ = ng	= o	= p	= qu	= r
= s	ᛏ = t	ᚦ = th	ᚢ = u	= v	= w	ᛉ = x	ᛦ = y	= z	

Writing

The Saxons could write using either ordinary letters or runes.
This sentence is written both ways.

His nama wæs Redwald ond his wifes nama wæs Ethelberga

Copy the table above. Use the Saxon sentence to draw in the missing runes.

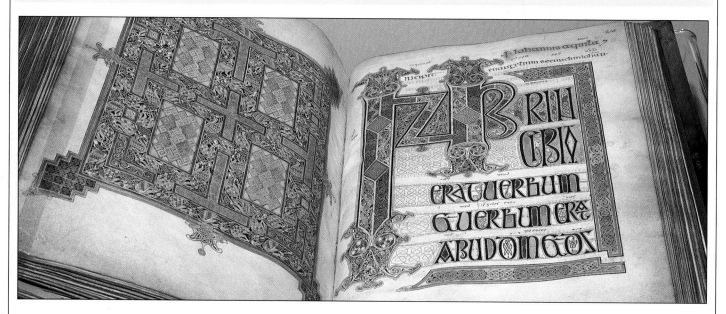

▲ Monks in monasteries sometimes turned letters into beautiful pictures.

Other invaders

▲ This priory was built by the Normans. The Normans were descended from Vikings.

About 300 years after the Saxons first began to settle in Britain, the Vikings started to raid the country. They attacked monasteries in the north of England, killing monks and stealing treasures. The raids continued. Eventually, the Vikings began to settle in Britain. They fought many battles against the Saxons.

Soon, the only Saxon kingdom left was Wessex. This jewel belonged to Alfred, who was the king of Wessex. The letters around the edge mean, 'Alfred had me made'.

We know quite a lot about what happened in Saxon times because the Saxons kept a book called the *Anglo-Saxon Chronicle.*

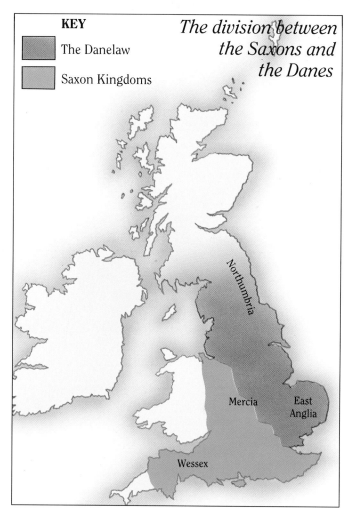

▲ This page from the *Chronicle* tells of a battle between Alfred and the Danish Vikings.

Eventually, the Saxons and the Vikings came to an agreement. The Saxons would rule Wessex and part of Mercia. The Vikings were to live in eastern and northern England. This area of England became known as the Danelaw.

▼ The map below shows where the Saxons and Vikings agreed to live.

KEY
The Danelaw
Saxon Kingdoms

The division between the Saxons and the Danes

Northumbria

Mercia

East Anglia

Wessex

Alfred had fortresses built just inside Wessex and the Saxon part of Mercia to make sure that the Vikings stayed out.

Many of the villages inside the fortresses grew into towns. The arrow on the photograph shows you one corner of a Saxon wall that was built around three sides of the town. A river protected the fourth side.

Place names

Lots of towns and villages got their names in Saxon times. They were often called after the crops that grew there or the animals that were kept there. Can you match the picture to the place name?

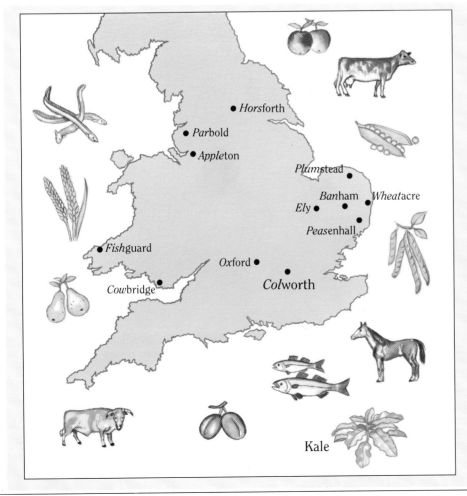

The Normans

Between AD 954 and AD 1066, Britain was ruled first by Saxons, then by Danes and then by Saxons once again.

In 1066, Duke William of Normandy and his army sailed over the sea to Britain. They fought a battle against the Saxon king, Harold. The Normans won. This battle became known as the Battle of Hastings.

▼ The story of how the Normans came to Britain is shown in a tapestry called the Bayeux Tapestry.

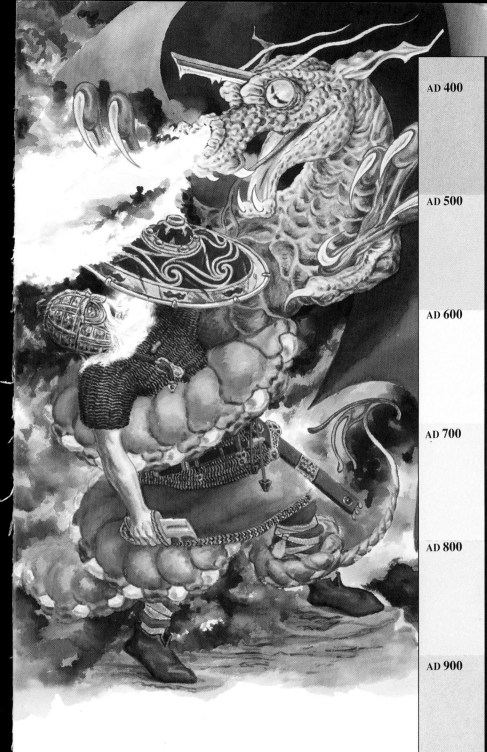

We have many reminders of the Saxons. Lots of our roads and towns date from Saxon times. We even know of a Saxon poem, called *Beowulf*, in which Beowulf fights monsters and dragons.

AD 400	The Romans leave Britain.
AD 500	Saxons begin to settle in England and southern Scotland.
	Christianity starts to spread across Britain.
AD 600	**624** The Sutton Hoo burials take place.
AD 700	
AD 800	**773** The Danes begin raiding.
	865 The Danes start to settle in England.
AD 900	**928** Alfred's son becomes king of England.
AD 1000	**1016** England is ruled by Danes.
	1042 England returns to Saxon rule.
AD 1100	**1066** The Saxons are defeated by the Normans at the Battle of Hastings.

Glossary

<u>archaeologists</u> People who dig up and study objects from the past in order to find out more about how people lived.

<u>fort</u> A type of castle with walls and ditches to keep out attackers.

<u>loom</u> A frame which people use to weave cloth to make clothes.

<u>monastery</u> A place where people live who choose to pray and obey strict rules because of what they believe about God.

<u>Normans</u> Warlike people from Normandy, which is a small area on the north coast of France. Led by Duke William, the Normans defeated the Saxons at the Battle of Hastings in 1066 and went on to rule England until 1150.

<u>Vikings</u> Warlike people from northern Europe – Norway, Sweden and Denmark – who crossed the North Sea to invade and settle in England in AD 793.

Books to read

Saxon Britain by Tony D. Triggs (Wayland, 1989)
Saxon Villages by Robin Place (Wayland, 1989)
The Anglo-Saxons by Roger Coote (Wayland, 1993)

Places to visit

If you would like to find out more about the Saxons, or see some remains of Saxon life, you could visit the following:

Churches, monasteries and cemeteries
Bradford-on-Avon, Wiltshire
Bradwell-on-Sea, Essex
Brixworth, Northamptonshire
Canterbury, Kent
Conisborough, South Yorkshire
Earls Barton, Northamptonshire
Escomb, County Durham
Iona, Strathclyde
Ledsham, West Yorkshire
Lindisfarne, Northumberland
North Elmham, Norfolk

Crosses
Bewcastle, Cumbria
Ilkley, West Yorkshire
Middleton, North Yorkshire
Ruthwell, Dumfriesshire
St Andrews, Fife
Whitby, North Yorkshire

Earthworks
Offa's Dyke, which is best seen north of Knighton, Powys.

Reconstructed Saxon huts
West Stow, near Bury St Edmunds, Suffolk.

Town defences
Wallingford, Oxfordshire
Wareham, Dorset

Museums
Ashmolean Museum, Oxford
Bede Monastery Museum, Jarrow
British Museum, London
Dumfries Museum, Dumfriesshire
Hull City Museum
Moyes Hall Museum, Bury St Edmunds
Museum of London
National Museum of Antiquities of Scotland, Edinburgh
Norwich Castle Museum
Sheffield City Museum
University Museum of Archaeology and Anthropology, Cambridge
Yorkshire Museum, York

Illustrated manuscripts
Durham Cathedral
Lichfield Cathedral

Index